GHOST HORSE

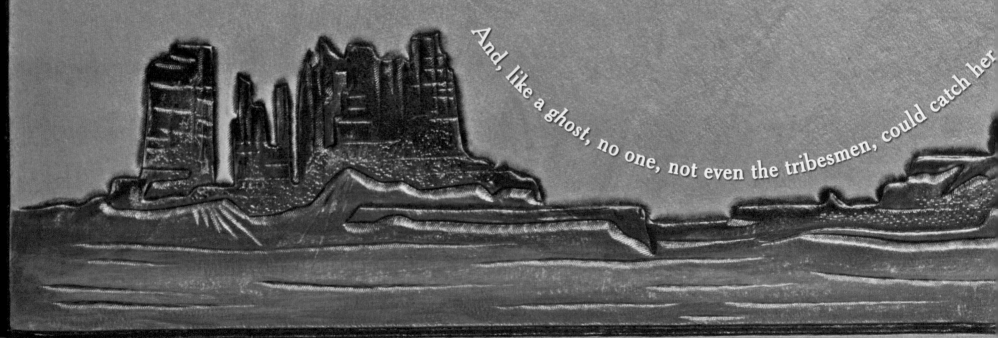

They called her Ghost Horse

And, like a ghost, no one, not even the tribesmen, could catch her

Still, in my dreams,
Ghost Horse and I
were riding together…

flying

across

the

night

sky.

Everyone in the tribe laughed
at me when I told them.

All except my grandmother.

She did not laugh.

She was a wise crone.

"A medicine woman," she said.

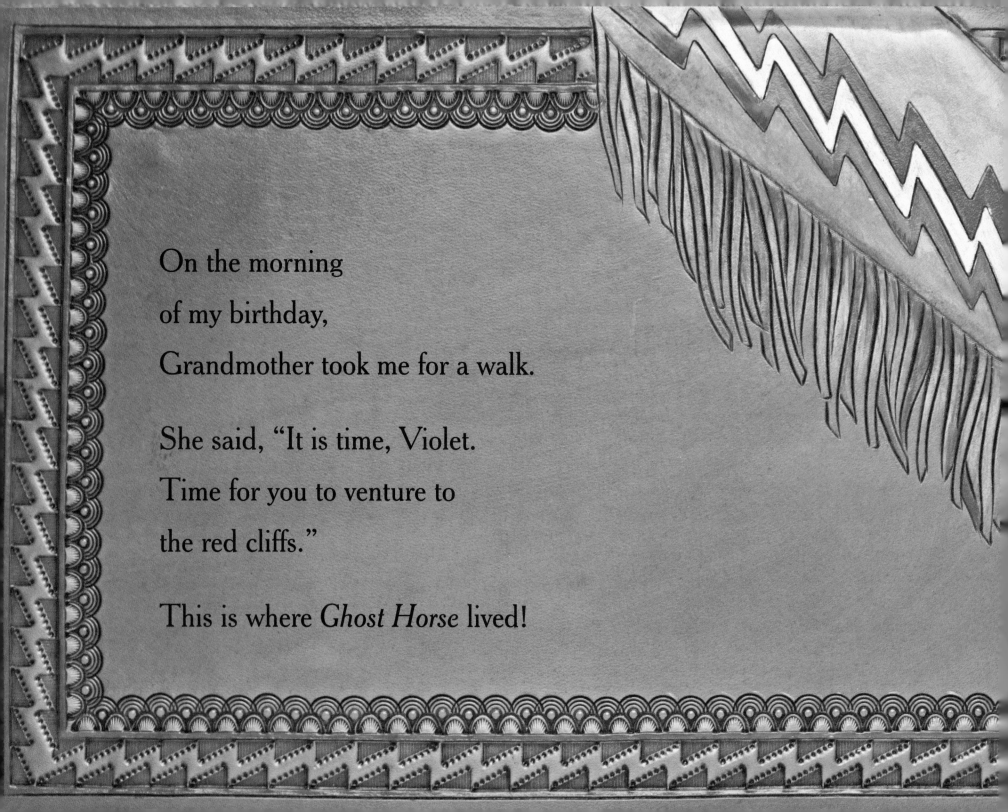

On the morning
of my birthday,
Grandmother took me for a walk.

She said, "It is time, Violet.
Time for you to venture to
the red cliffs."

This is where *Ghost Horse* lived!

We watched her
from far away.

I asked,

"But why are we going there?

The men say we cannot outrun her."

Grandmother said,

"They are right. So we will not chase her."

Instead, we watched her,

being as quiet and still as possible.

pulled the squash into her mouth.

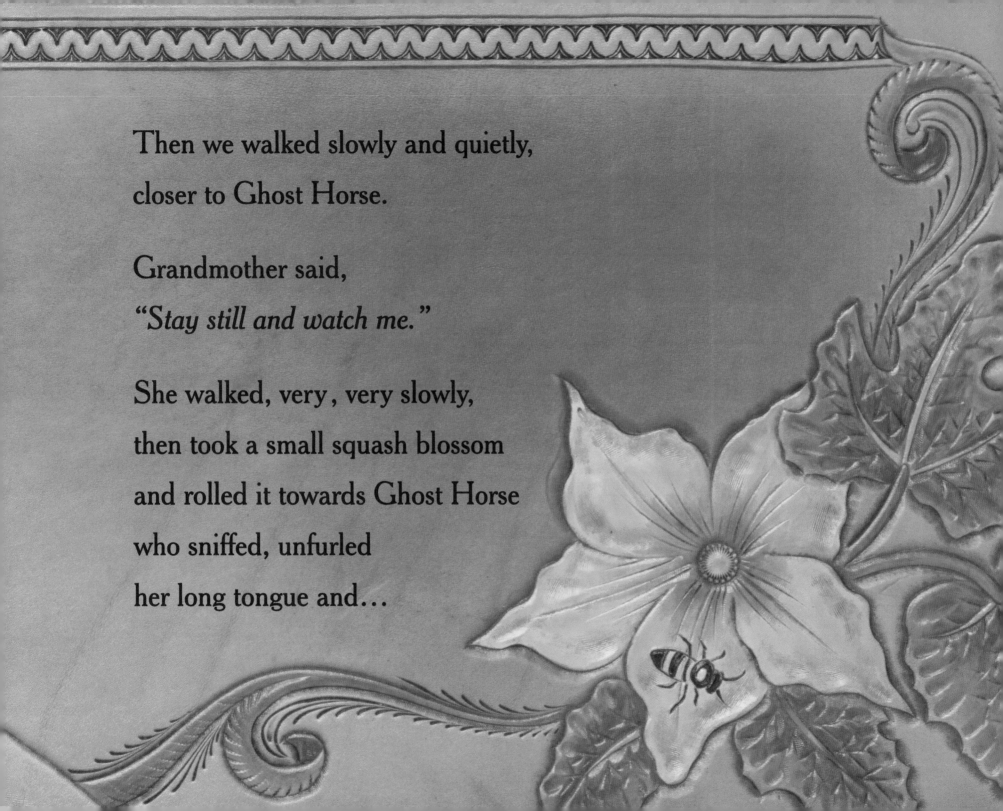

Then we walked slowly and quietly,

closer to Ghost Horse.

Grandmother said,

"Stay still and watch me."

She walked, very, very slowly,

then took a small squash blossom

and rolled it towards Ghost Horse

who sniffed, unfurled

her long tongue and…

Ghost Horse sniffed her hand,
then let out a huge sigh.

Grandmother was not afraid.

She was a healer.

When someone in the tribe was sick, she
would know which flowers and plants would
help them feel better.

She touched the horse lightly on her head, then stroked its long white front leg

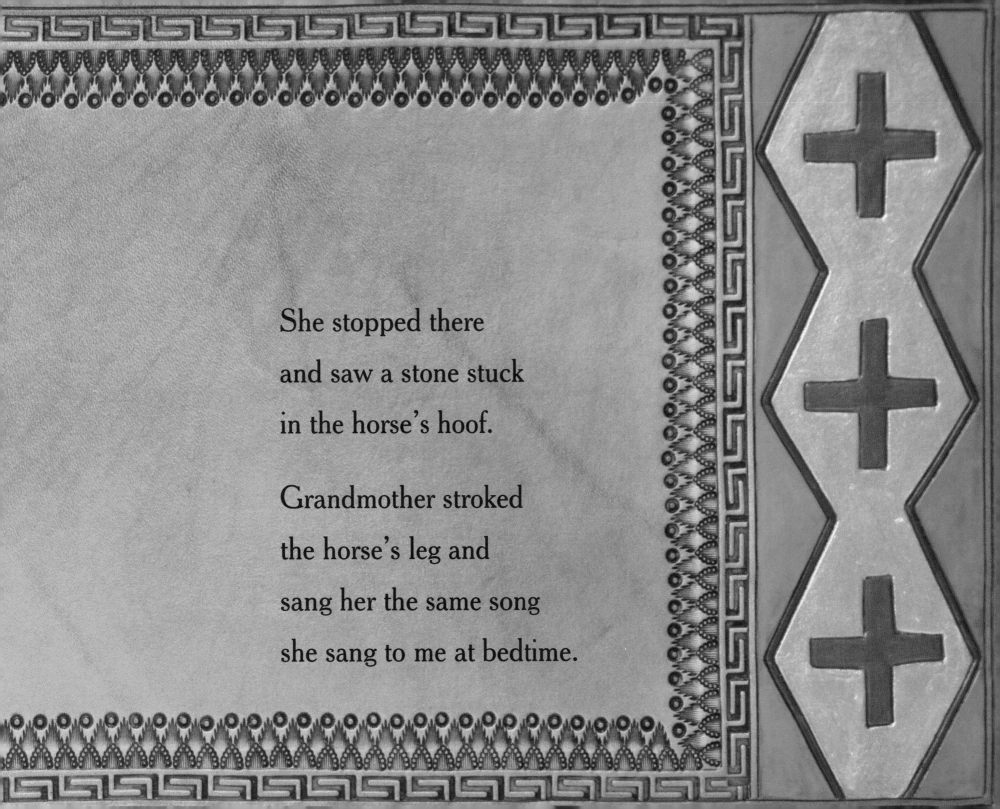

She stopped there
and saw a stone stuck
in the horse's hoof.

Grandmother stroked
the horse's leg and
sang her the same song
she sang to me at bedtime.

"close your eyes, close your eyes, dream world comes and spirit flies, spirit flies to the skies, on eagle's wings to sunrise. "

Ghost Horse fell asleep. Grandmother gently pulled the stone from the hoof. Then she took leaves and sticky bush sap and pressed them in where the stone had been. She lay her hand on the hoof until a crow cried, and whispered into the horse's ear something I could not hear.

I asked her, *"Were you afraid, being so close to a ghost?"*

"She is not a ghost, Violet. She is alive, like you and I, and she needed help."

caw! caw!

"When any living thing needs help we give it."

I asked, "What did you say to her?"

For a long time she said nothing.

Then she said, "It is our secret. Maybe she will tell you someday."

The next day, when Grandmother held out her hand with a squash, the horse walked slowly up to her, bowed her head and took the offering.

I did not move.
I was still afraid.

Then Ghost
Horse moved
her head to me
and sniffed.

I could feel her warm breath
on my cheek and it tickled.

She looked at me. Her eyes were big
and blue, like the sky. I had never seen such
eyes. Her breath tickled me again, and this
time I thought I saw Ghost Horse smile, too.

Ghost Horse looked me
in the eye as if she wanted
to tell me something
I did not yet understand.

Just then, I heard yelling
and turned to see the tribesmen.
They had returned on another
chase. . . . .

Ghost Horse bolted!

Grandmother spoke,
"Just as my mother said:
'If you chase a dream, it will fly
away from you.' Thus she has flown
away, dear Violet."

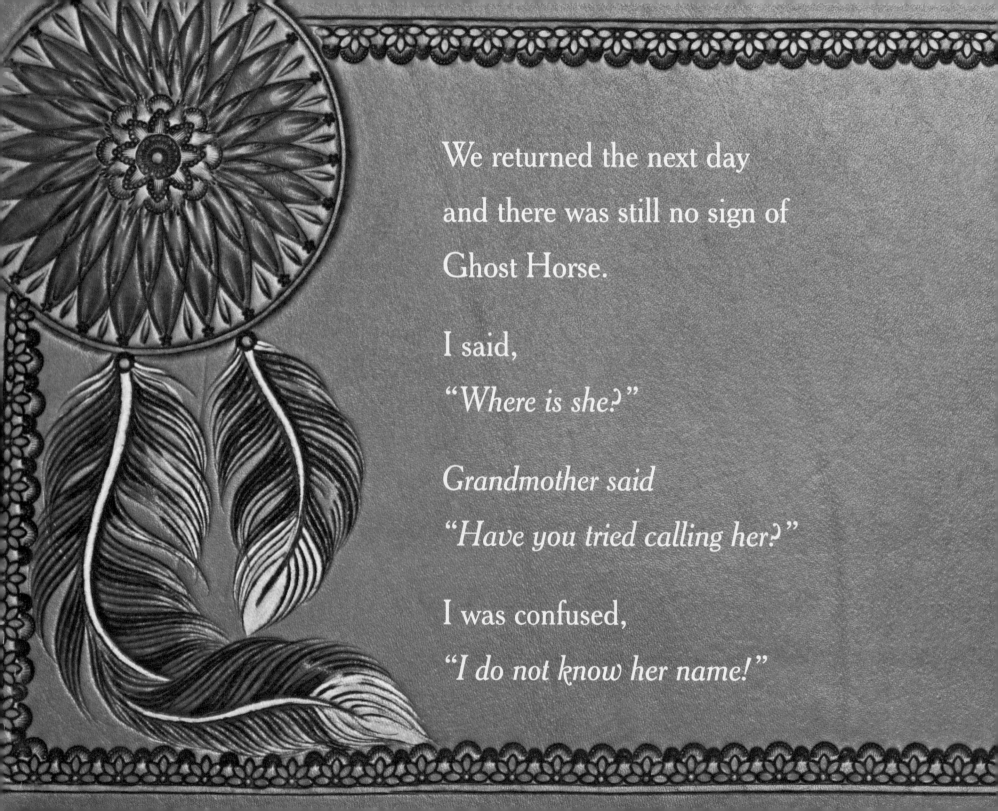

We returned the next day
and there was still no sign of
Ghost Horse.

I said,

"Where is she?"

Grandmother said
"Have you tried calling her?"

I was confused,

"I do not know her name!"

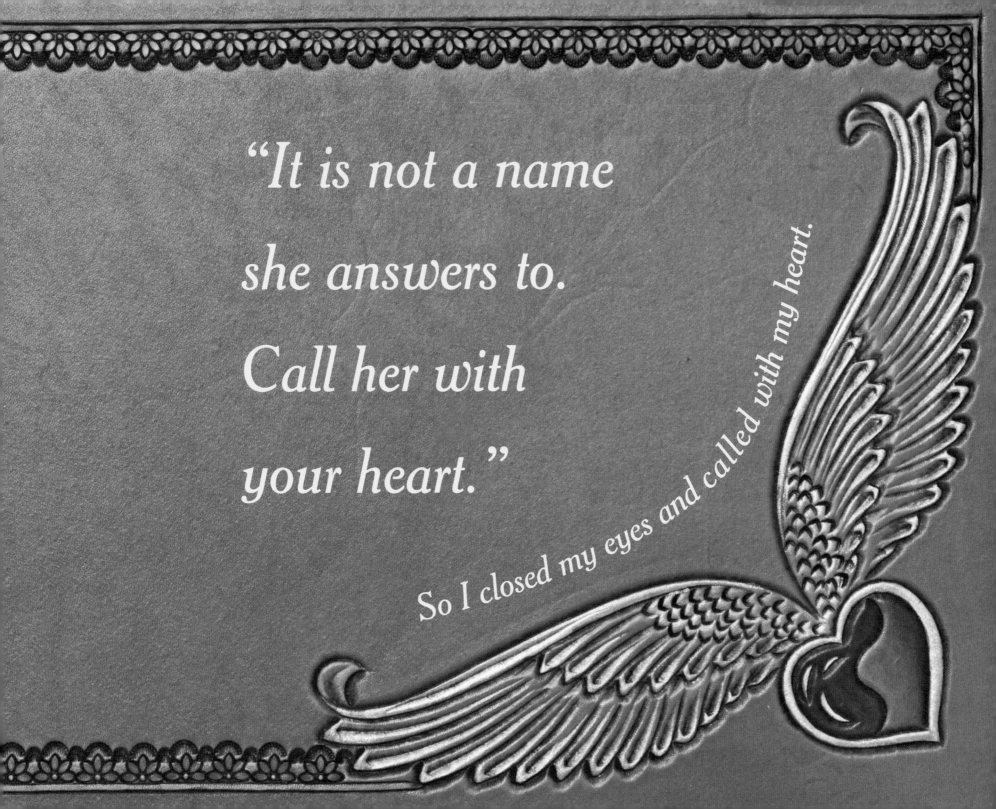

"It is not a name she answers to. Call her with your heart."

So I closed my eyes and called with my heart.

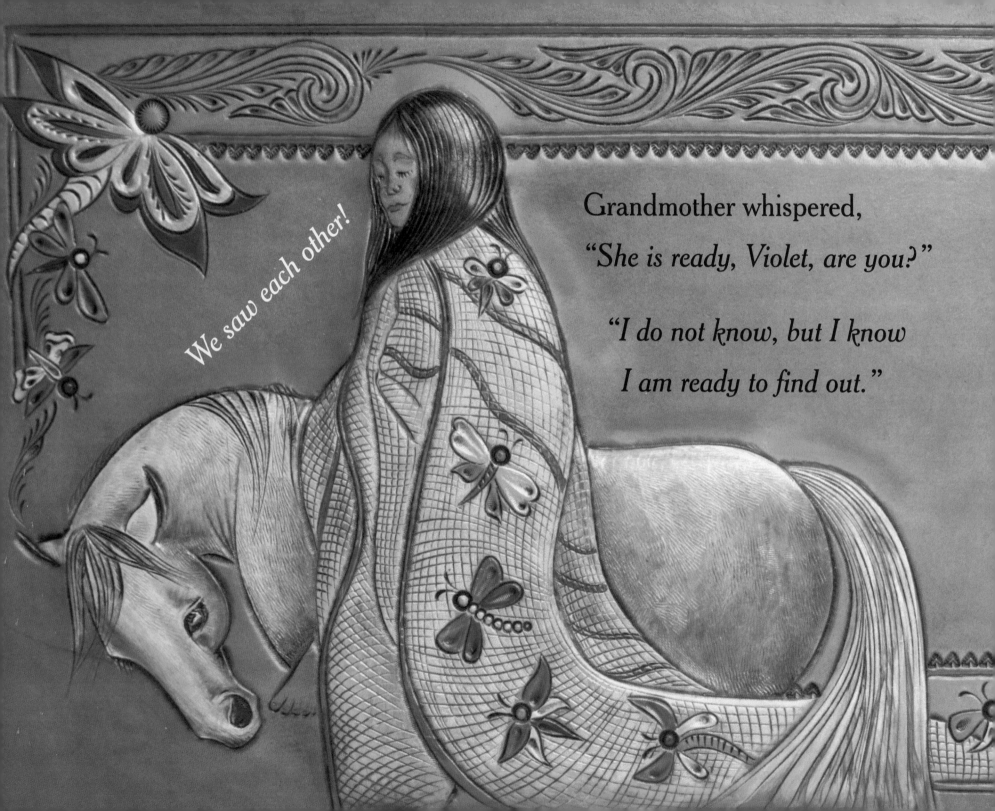

We saw each other!

Grandmother whispered,
"She is ready, Violet, are you?"

"I do not know, but I know
I am ready to find out."

I put my hand on Ghost Horse's mane and stroked her gently, then held tight and pulled myself up onto her back. Her hair tickled my legs. She turned her head and looked at me with her big blue eyes. I looked right back at her. *We saw each other.*

I was *not* afraid. Then Ghost Horse let a snort and began to walk!

Grandmother called out, *"Hold onto her mane. Hold on tight!"*

Ghost Horse's mane was very strong and I held on with both hands.

Then I did what I had seen others do — I squeezed my legs gently.

She made a gruff noise, and I said, *"It is fine, my friend, I am with you."*

She began to trot. Then, without warning, she broke into a gallop! I had never gone this fast, like the wind. I was afraid, but also excited. Where was she going? I held on tight. I felt like we were flying.

Then I remembered that if I pressed my heel against the horse in the direction I wanted to go, she would go that way. I guided her towards the pueblo.

Her mane was shining in the sun as she took happy steps, like she was dancing. Now that she was no longer a ghost, she needed a good name.

I shall call you Sundance

When we reached the pueblo,
everyone stood around silently.

Grandmother came out of the crowd
and announced to everyone,
*"Look how our brave girl
did what none of you could do!"*   Sundance bowed to them.

The Tribesmen ran towards us, but we flew away.
They could never catch us.

From then on we were together.
Spending our days flying.

One day I asked Sundance what
Grandmother had said to her
so long ago.

I put my hand on Sundance's neck,
and looked into her eyes…

I listened with my heart and heard her say, "With this girl you can fly."

And that is where I got my name, Sky Horse.

Years passed—I taught the other girls to ride. We became mothers. We taught our children what we had learned.

Our children taught it to their children and now I pass it on to you.

"If you chase a dream, it will fly away from you.

But if you give it love,
it will fly away with you."

DEDICATION

To *Violet* and *Jett*

from their Grandma *(Yaya)*

Grandpa *(Oda)*

and Uncle DD

May our magic
and love

infuse your lives
and dreams!

Lisa Skyhorse, Illustrations

Lisa and Loren Skyhorse, www.Skyhorse.com are an internationally recognized Saddle Making team for over 40 years. They are famous for their one-of-a-kind, contemporary work that elevates leather work to an art form.

The illustrations in this book were hand carved and painted on leather by Lisa, many incorporating a hand-sculpted process.

Lisa and Loren have two children, Ocea and Ari, and two grandchildren, Violet and Jett. They live and work in Durango, Colorado with their 5 horses, two dogs and two cats.

Daniel Will-Harris, Writer

Daniel Will-Harris is an internationally-recognized best-selling author, teacher, and designer. He's developed plays with the Kennedy Center Playwriting Intensive and MoMA calls his designs "truly unique." He's written 8 books (selling over 300,000 copies), three feature film screenplays, and over 600 short stories currently featured in his popular story podcast, www.Anchor.fm/WriteNowStories

Will-Harris created and wrote the book on his *Write in the Now* process www.WriteInTheNow.com. He teaches writers and artists to discover endless ideas, eliminate writer's block, find passion in their projects, and get to the very heart of their work.

www.SKYHORSE.COM

WRITEINTHENOW.COM

COPYRIGHT

WALDEMAR WINKLER - PHOTOGRAPHER

Waldemar's passion for photography started while a
teenager with a class taught by Ferenc Berko.
Photography, along with video, were constant
companions in his career as a media specialist in the
meetings and conventions industry. He continues
to explore the many paths of photo expression.
His work can be seen at:
WWW.FLICKR.COM/PHOTOS/TWOFISHPHOTO

Thanks to:

Peter Bramley and Beth Lockhart
and *Pants On Fire Theater*, London